The Court of Appeals at Austin

1892 - 1992

BY

DEBORAH D. POWERS

STATE HOUSE PRESS
Austin, Texas
1992

Library of Congress Cataloging-in-Publication Data

Powers, Deborah D. (Deborah Daniels). 1942-
The Court of Appeals at Austin : 1892-1992 /
by Deborah D. Powers.
p. cm.
Includes bibliographical references.
ISBN 0-938349-92-9 (hardcover : alk. paper)
1. Texas. Court of Appeals (3rd)—History. 2. Appellate courts—Texas—History. 3. Judges—Texas—History.
I. Texas. Court of Appeals (3rd) II. Title

KFT1714.T47P68 1992
347.764'03—dc20
[347.64073] 92-28116

—Limited to 500 copies—

Printed in the United States of America

STATE HOUSE PRESS
P.O. Box 15247
Austin, Texas 78761

To John

and to my mother

Nadine Sheldon Daniels

ACKNOWLEDGEMENTS

Many people have helped make this book possible. Some are direct descendants of the justices: Flora Clarke Nevitt of Houston, granddaughter of Justice Streetman, who sent valuable photographs, and her son Rodney Nevitt; John R. Streetman of Victoria, Texas; Dr. Sam Key, Jr., a second-generation eye surgeon in Austin who practices medicine with his son, Dr. Sam Key; Adele Belvin of Brownwood who entrusted me with copies of family documents and photographs to provide information on Justice Baugh; Lois and Charles Archer who loaned me their copy of a family history, *The Legacy of John McQuatty Archer,* compiled by grandson Coleman J. Archer; Coleman J. Archer who kindly permitted me to copy excerpts from his book; W.E. Eidson who provided me copies of family documents; Diane Grant who was married to Justice Rice's grandson, gave me both information and an introduction to three of Justice Rice's surviving children; Mary Carter Rice, Elizabeth Rice Finks and Emily Rice Finch who graciously shared their memories with a stranger; Howard Richards, Justice C.K. Richard's son; Catherine Tyson of Dallas, Justice Archer's daughter, and her son, attorney Knox Tyson; Trueman O'Quinn, Jr.; and William Edwin Collard, a distant cousin of Justice Collard, who supplied his family's genealogy and family letters.

Bill Fowler and Dr. Jenny Lind Porter shared their memories of Justice O'Quinn; Judge Frank Maloney of the Court of Criminal Appeals and Joan Smith took time to review Justice Smith's biographical sketch; Henry and Kay Brooks helped me locate Justice Fisher's great-grandson, William Jones of Idaho; Clinton Morse of Andrews & Kurth provided much of the information on Justice Streetman; Margo Scogin shared her recollections of Justice John W. Brady and tried to put me in touch with his relatives; and Irene Varan, Chair of the Williamson County Historical Committee, examined Williamson County census records for me.

Cynthia Freeman and Angela Dorau, of the Governor Bill and Vara Daniel Center for Legal History at the State Bar of Texas, were very helpful in gathering information on all of the justices. Bonnie Campbell of the State Preservation Board, Bill Kennedy and John Anderson of the State Archives, and Michael Widener at the Tarlton Law Library, The University of Texas School of Law, also provided valuable assistance.

Charlotte Kidd gathered the photographs of the twenty-eight justices and chose the ones used in the book. Her skills and support meant a great deal to me. Also generous in their support of the project were Madelon Carroll and Linda Jones who gathered information on several of the justices, and Susan Bage and Kenneth Law who provided me early court documents.

My husband John contributed to my education on family research by, among other things, telling me about the death records at the State Archives—after I returned home, exhausted and covered with burs, from searching for tombstones on a scorching summer day in an old Austin cemetery. John was also a valuable editor and, as always, supportive of my efforts.

Tom Munnerlyn, Erik Mason and Debbie Brothers of State House Press provided enthusiastic support and were a pleasure to work with.

To these individuals who have so willingly and generously assisted me, I am forever grateful.

FOREWORD

The State of Texas is divided into fourtees districts, each with a court of appeals that hears appeals taken from trial courts within the district. From the decisions of these courts, the Supreme Court of Texas may grant further review in civil cases. In criminal cases the Texas Court of Criminal Appeals may do the same. Generally speaking, these two highest state courts will hear appeals only from the courts of appeals.

The Court of Appeals at Austin serves the Third District of Texas, a district composed of twenty-four central-Texas counties that lie on or near the Colorado River. The counties range from Sterling County in West Texas to Fayette County in the east, and from Bell County in the north to Comal County in the south. These twenty-four counties comprise 20,470 square miles and contain a population well over one million.

In addition to serving a large geographic area, the Court of Appeals at Austin hears numerous cases in which the state or one of its agencies is a party. For this reason the Court of Appeals at Austin has long been known as a specialist in "administrative law," or that part of the law dealing with the administration of state government. These administrative-law cases involve most aspects of state government, from utility and transportation rates to oil and gas regulation to air and water quality. In its decisions in such cases, the Court of Appeals at Austin serves the entire state.

Twenty-eight justices, including the six who presently serve, have sat on the court since it was established in 1892, one hundred years ago. This book honors the centennial of the court with a collection of biographical sketches of those justices and related information, including rosters of the court clerks, law clerks and staff attorneys who have served the court so ably.

The biographical sketches reveal long and distinguished careers. Justice William Mercer Key, one of the three original justices selected for the court in 1892, served on the court for over thirty-one years. Three of the justices served together for twenty-three consecutive years during which time they laid the foundation of the state's administrative law and became known as "The Great Triumvirate" owing to their scholarship and fairness. The sketches also suggest sadness and loss—the election defeat of a great judge at a time before state judges received pensions—and even tragedy: Justice John Brady, seven years after he left the court, was found guilty of murder and served three years in prison for his crime.

Long life and happiness stand out as well. Justice James McClendon lived to age ninety-eight and enjoyed twenty-three years of very active retirement after serving twenty-five years on the court. Justice Benjamin Herbert Rice, who died in 1918, is survived by four of his nine children, aged eighty-seven to ninety-four.

The justices have several similarities in background as well as interesting differences. Six of them were district or county judges before taking their seats on the Court of Appeals at Austin; three were both district and county judges. Ten of the justices had never held public office before serving on the court. Seventeen came to the court by gubernatorial appointment. Only three of the twenty-eight justices lost their seats by election defeats.

Two of the justices fought in the Civil War, one at age sixteen. Two others served in both World War I and in World War II.

All but nine of the twenty-eight justices were graduates of the law department (1883-1920) or the School of Law at The University of Texas at Austin. Six of the justices never attended law school but were admitted to the bar after reading law in Texas and South Carolina law offices.

Justice Roy Archer was United States Commissioner and permit agent for the Slavic States following World War I. Justice Mallory Benton Blair served as a judge on a military tribunal at Nuremberg for the trial of German war criminals, including German judges. Justice Trueman O'Quinn was a recognized authority on the famous author O. Henry.

There have been important firsts. Justice Bob Smith, a former Democratic district attorney, was the first Republican to serve on the court following a gubernatorial appointment in 1980. In 1986 Justice Marilyn Aboussie became the first woman to sit on the court. In 1991 Justice Bob Gammage became the first justice from the Court of Appeals at Austin to serve on the Supreme Court of Texas.

It has been a privilege to be associated with the Court of Appeals at Austin and a pleasure to search out the available information on the lives of the early justices. Texas has had many distinguished jurists, and more than a few of them have served on the Court of Appeals at Austin.

Deborah D. Powers
August 1992

COURTROOM OF THE COURT OF APPEALS
AT AUSTIN, 1992.
Photos courtesy of the Archives Division, Texas State Library.

THE APPELLATE COURTS OF TEXAS

> The right of appeal within reasonable limits is a highly important one. The people of the State have been habituated to it and would not likely surrender it. They will not consent to a system which ignores it....The [court] system is, therefore, one founded on experience; and more than that, it has been evolved out of necessity. Despite its imperfections, it is one seasoned with years of honorable and arduous service in behalf of the people. In the larger view it has bravely met and faithfully borne the burdens imposed by the severe demands of the widespread litigation of a rapidly growing state.
>
> —The Honorable Nelson Phillips,
> 1 Texas Jurisprudence, p. xxxviii

The basic structure of the Texas court system has remained essentially unchanged since Texas became a republic in 1836. The changes that have been made have been largely in the appellate courts.

UNDER THE REPUBLIC

The Constitution of the Republic of Texas, adopted March 17, 1836, established the judicial department by providing for a supreme court, district courts, county courts, justice courts, and such other inferior courts as the legislature might create. The constitution assigned appellate jurisdiction to the district courts to review certain cases from the county courts, but the only exclusively appellate court was the supreme court. It had jurisdiction of both civil and criminal appeals and reviewed questions of fact as well as questions of law. The court consisted of a chief justice, who could not be a member of any other court, and not more than eight associate justices who were also judges of the several district courts of the Republic.

In addition, the judicial article called upon congress to introduce by legislation the common law of England with such modification as circumstances required in the judgment of congress. This was done in an act of January 24, 1840, when the common law was made the rule of decision, with certain exceptions. A notable exception was that the property rights of husband and wife would be governed by the civil, not common, law.

The "Supreme Court of the Republic of Texas" met for the first time January 19, 1840. It was an itinerant court that was permitted to meet once each year at two places other than the state capital and Congress filled all judicial offices by a joint vote.

UNDER THE STATE

The State Constitutions of 1845, 1861, 1866 and 1869 retained the same basic court structure, although the manner of selecting supreme court judges and the length of their terms changed with each constitution. In the final Constitution of 1876, the number of justices was initially set at three (now nine), they were to serve a term of six years, and all judicial offices were required to be filled by popular elections.

With 1,600 cases pending before the supreme court by 1875, the Constitution of 1876 added a second appellate court, the Court of Appeals, and gave it jurisdiction in all criminal appeals and in civil appeals arising from cases tried in the county courts. The Supreme Court of Texas retained appellate jurisdiction in cases tried in the district courts but had no criminal jurisdiction.

The Court of Appeals, with almost exclusive criminal jurisdiction, was the first of its kind ever established. Today only two other courts of appeal have criminal jurisdiction only, the Court of Criminal Appeals of England, created by an Act of Parliament in 1907, and the Criminal Court of Appeals in Oklahoma, established in 1908.

To further relieve the appellate docket, in an act of July 9, 1879, the legislature created a Commission of Arbitration and Award which would hear civil cases referred from the supreme court or the Court of Appeals by consent of the parties. To sustain the constitutionality of the legislation, the supreme court held that the commission did not constitute a "court" but was rather a board of arbitration without the power to render a binding decision. A later statute in 1881 required that the commission submit its decisions to the supreme court for adoption, rejection, or approval and that the supreme court and the Court of Appeals might, on their own motion, refer civil cases to the commission. The commission was restyled the Commission of Appeals.

In 1885 the legislature allowed the Commission of Appeals to expire. It was reestablished in 1887, but only to review appeals pending before the supreme court. In 1891 the legislature expanded the commission to six judges, but the appellate system could not keep pace with the number of appeals. The number of district courts had increased to fifty-three from the original eight during the days of the Republic.

It was necessary either to limit appeals drastically or to provide additional courts for their determination. The legislature chose the latter, and in its regular session in 1891 proposed an amendment to the constitution to give the legislature power to create additional appellate courts. In August 1891 the citizens of Texas approved the amendment, and on April 13, 1892, an act was approved in special session that divided the state into three supreme judicial districts and established in each an intermediate appellate court: the First Court of Civil Appeals at Galveston, the Second Court of Civil Appeals at Fort Worth, and the Third Court of Civil Appeals at Austin.

The 1891 amendment changed the Court of Appeals to

the Court of Criminal Appeals and made its appellate jurisdiction exclusive in criminal cases; it retained no jurisdiction over any civil cases. The Commission of Appeals was abolished and four of the six judges on the commission became justices on the three courts of civil appeals: C.C. Garrett became Chief Justice on the First Court at Galveston; B.D. Tarlton, Chief Justice on the Second Court at Fort Worth; and H.C. Fisher, Chief Justice, and W.E. Collard, one of the associate justices, on the Third Court at Austin.

The jurisdiction of the courts of civil appeals extended to civil cases only; it was exclusively appellate and limited to cases involving more than a specified sum. The review of questions of fact in the supreme court was limited to the legal sufficiency of the evidence, the factual sufficiency of the evidence being placed exclusively in the new courts of civil appeals. This did not mean that the new courts might find facts themselves, but that they might determine whether there was sufficient evidence to support the explicit or implied fact-findings necessary to the trial court judgment. In addition, the judgments of the courts of civil appeals were made conclusive on both questions of fact and on questions of law in certain specified kinds of cases, such as divorce and slander. In general, however, litigants in the court of civil appeals were entitled to appeal to the supreme court by writ of error, except in the specified cases.

The amendment of 1891 further provided that the number of courts of civil appeals should be increased by the legislature in accordance with "the increase of population and business." Only a year later, the legislature created two additional supreme judicial districts, one for the Fourth Court of Civil Appeals at San Antonio and the Fifth Court of Civil Appeals at Dallas. Nine additional Courts of Civil Appeals followed: in 1907 the Sixth Court of Civil Appeals at Texarkana; in 1911 the Seventh and Eighth Courts of Civil Appeals at Amarillo and El Paso, respectively; in 1915 the Ninth Court of Civil Appeals at Beaumont; in 1923 the Tenth Court of Civil Appeals at Waco; in 1925 the Eleventh Court of Civil Appeals at Eastland; and in 1963 the Twelfth and Thirteenth Courts of Civil Appeals at

Tyler and Corpus Christi, respectively. In 1957 the First Court of Civil Appeals was moved from Galveston to Houston and in 1967 the legislature created another court to sit at Houston, the Fourteenth Court of Civil Appeals.

On September 1, 1981, by constitutional amendment, the courts of civil appeals received criminal jurisdiction for the first time. This was done to relieve the large backlog that existed at the Court of Criminal Appeals. The courts of civil appeals were renamed courts of appeals.

The 1981 amendment also provided that in death penalty cases the appellate jurisdiction of the Court of Criminal Appeals was to remain exclusive. In all other cases the basis for appeal to the Court of Criminal Appeals was the same as for the supreme court: appeals based on legal error in the Court of Appeal's judgment.

During the past ten years, 55 percent of new cases filed in the courts of appeals have been criminal cases.

QUALIFICATIONS TO SERVE ON A COURT OF APPEALS

The term of office is six years beginning January 1. No person is eligible to the office unless he or she is licensed to practice law in Texas, is at the time of election a citizen of the United States and Texas, has attained the age of thirty-five years, is a resident of the district from which he or she is elected, and has been a practicing lawyer, or a lawyer and judge of a court of record, at least ten years. If a vacancy occurs on a court of appeals, the governor fills the vacancy until the next general election, and at the general election the vacancy for the unexpired term is filled through election by the qualified voters of the district.

THE CENTENNIAL COURT

Back row, from left to right: Justice Mack Kidd; Justice Marilyn Aboussie; Justice Bea Ann Smith; Justice Woodie Jones. Seated: Chief Justice Jimmy Carroll (left) and Justice John Powers.
Photo by John Jefferson.

THE COURT OF APPEALS AT AUSTIN

The Court of Civil Appeals at Austin met formally for the first time October 3, 1892. Cases were first submitted to the court October 7, 1892, and its first opinions were announced and filed October 19, 1892. At that time the state was divided into three supreme judicial districts, and the Third District for the Court of Civil Appeals at Austin consisted of seventy-three counties. Today there are fourteen district courts of appeal, and the Third District consists of twenty-four central-Texas counties: Bastrop, Bell, Blanco, Burnet, Caldwell, Coke, Comal, Concho, Fayette, Hays, Irion, Lampasas, Lee, Llano, McCulloch, Milam, Mills, Runnels, San Saba, Schleicher, Sterling, Tom Green, Travis, and Williamson. About half of all appeals originate in Travis County.

For sixty-seven years the Court of Civil Appeals at Austin was located in the capitol. In January 1960 the court moved to the ground floor of the newly-built Supreme Court Building just west of the capitol. In 1981, though the courtroom remained in the Supreme Court Building, the justices' and clerks' offices were moved to the adjoining eight-story tower that was built at the same time as the Supreme Court Building. In May 1991 the courtroom and the justices' offices were moved to the new Price Daniel, Sr. Building at the corner of West Fourteenth and Lavaca Streets.

In 1982 the Court of Appeals at Austin increased from three justices to six justices. The increase was to accommodate the transfer of criminal cases to the court and in accordance with the constitutional amendment adopted in 1978 that allowed the legislature to increase the number of justices as the workload demanded. Three new justices stood for election in 1982. The three candidates who won the Democratic primary and were unopposed in the general election took office four months early, by gubenatorial appointment, on September 1, 1982.

CLERKS OF THE COURT

The court has had nine clerks of the court, appointed by the court to two-year terms. Duties include recording the judgments, decrees, decisions, and orders of the court, filing and carefully preserving the transcripts of all records certified to the court and all related papers, and maintaining the docket of all causes in the order in which they are filed. The clerk is also responsible for maintaining the court library and for providing a biannual account of all court costs collected and disposed of. The nine clerks are listed below as their names appear in the court minutes.

Will L. Vining	1892-1896
R.H. Connerly	1896-1932
S.A. Philquist	1932-1934
R.E. Moore	1934-1947
Mrs. R. E. Moore	1947-1962
Mrs. Maurice Woodland	1962-1972
Mrs. Margie Love	1972-1985
Susan K. Bage	1985-1991
W. Kenneth Law	1991-

LAW CLERKS

In 1971 the Court of Civil Appeals at Austin began to employ law clerks to assist the justices with legal research. The law clerks serve for a one-year term beginning the first working day in September.

The court presently engages six law clerks. Each of the six is assigned to the justice who selected him or her through an application-interview process that took place about a year previously. Competition for the law-clerk positions is quite keen, and there are typically many more applicants than positions. The clerks finally chosen by the justices have usually proved themselves to be very good law students with high grades. Almost invariably they are newly graduated from law school but not yet licensed to practice law because they have yet to learn, in September, whether they have passed the bar examination that most have taken in the summer immediately preceding their employment. The first month as a law clerk is marked by a certain undercurrent of tension concerning the results of the bar examination.

In the year of employment that commences in September, the clerk and the justice for whom he or she works are in a close partnership as they carry together their share of the court's workload. In the beginning both wonder whether they have made a wise decision—the justice being apprehensive about how his or her choice will actually turn out, the new clerk laboring under a doubt about his or her ability to do the work well, and both having more than a little curiosity about the other's personal and professional qualities and how the two of them will get along for a year in a close working relationship. Will the first day be the high-water mark, followed by a deteriorating relationship as the year passes so that both are relieved when the torment is ended on the clerk's last working day; or will the last day leave a firm friendship based solidly on mutual respect and affection? It is easy to imagine the worst that first month. In most instances the early fears are groundless.

In the ensuing year the clerk assists his or her justice in about forty appeals that have been more or less difficult. The two have not, however, tended merely to the necessary legal research and writing that results in suggested opinions for the court in those forty appeals. They have done these basic things, of course, but they have also spent a good deal of time encouraging each other in their work and exchanging views about a wide range of other matters: customs and ethics in the practice of law; the less well-known places to find the law; how law is made and understood; the importance of law in society; and any number of other topics that may have nothing to do with a particular appeal but bear in a general way upon all appeals that come to the court or that have to do with cases that may confront a clerk when he or she becomes a practicing lawyer. This is a two-way street; a justice learns as much as he or she imparts to the clerk. Both the justice and the clerk become better legal scholars in consequence, just as they become better friends in the process. Ninety-six law clerks have contributed to the work of the court:

1971

James Wayne Minor

1972

William Thomas Blanton

1973

Robert Whitehill

1974

Charles Blackley

1975

Maurice Walton
Ralph K. Harrison
Gale Michael Fjetland

1976

Robert Cross
Ulysses Samuel Jones
Russell J. Light

1977

Michael Boyle
Luis Chavez
William Fowler

1978

Gary Buckwalter
Chris Hale
David C. Duggins

1979

Frank C. Davis, III
Louis A. Silverman
Richard Crozier

1980

James Ewbank, II
Rodney G. Ellis
Mary Hover McCarthy
Carl F. Baker

1981

Michael R. Klatt
Madeleine E. Dabney
Grant Kaiser
Michael C. Klein
J. Stephen Ravel
Nancy K. Matchus

1982

Robert D. "Bobby" Stokes
James S. Witherspoon
Michael J. Booth
Steven E. Rogers
Brian J. Brandstetter
Linda B. Secord

1983

Gina V. Fulkerson
Gary L. Steel
Stephen F. Morris
Christina L. Lewis
Blanca A. Uzeta-O'Leary
James D. Walker

1984

Theodore G. Mishtal
George B. Slade
Lisa L. Bagley-Brown
Cynthia D. Swartz
John T. Fleming
John T. Raba

1985

Kerry P. McGrath
Lancelot P. Olinde, Jr.
Gregory L. Watkins
Philip T. Houser
Carter C. White
Cheri Witter

1986

John F. Williams
Kenneth G. Mahaffey
Nancy McCluskey Green
A. Scott Campbell
Michael W. Eady
Nissa L. Mykelby

1987

Stuart Whitlow
Sandra K. Honath
Brett Campbell
Matthew L. Trevena
William D. Dugat, III
Karin Bonicoro

1988

John Greytok
Margaret Uhlig
Susan Ayres
Dean Schaffer
Kristen A. Algert
Carolyn Porter Simone

1989

Jan Tierney	Chris Reeder
Cheryl Ann Schultz	E. Scott Polikov
Joe Freeland	Sharmyn Lumsden

1990

Holly Claghorn	Chris Elliott
Amanda Foote	Terry Hammond
Caroline LeGette	Karen L. Watkins
Margaret Menicucci	

1991

Jerry V. Beard	Christine L. Hannah
Gina M. Lambert	Walter G. Mattison
Ron Moss	Kimberley K. Waterhouse

1992

Charles C. Finch	Julian Grant
Caroline Kelley	Pamela Moore
Lisa Paulson	Timothy D. Ryan

STAFF ATTORNEYS

Since 1981 when the legislature first authorized a single staff attorney, the court has employed sixteen lawyers in staff positions. The first was Charles Blackley, a former law clerk for the court. Three other former staff attorneys were also former law clerks: Robert D. "Bobbie" Stokes, James S. Witherspoon and Brian J. Brandstetter. The other former staff attorneys are Lisa Gilbreath, Craig D. Spirduso, Carol Ann Wood, William P. Green, Anne S. Lewis and Jeff Smith. The six staff attorneys who presently serve the court are Cheri Witter and Karin Bonicoro, both former law clerks, Pat Shannon, Jessie Amos, Emmy Edwards and Charles Spain, Jr.

The staff attorneys assist the justices in resolving the many legal problems that attend the numerous appeals taken to the court. Without their scholarly efforts, the time required to dispose of such appeals would lengthen considerably because there are so many appeals taken.

Biographical Sketches

H. C. Fisher

Tom Green County

1892-1910

H.C. Fisher

H.C. Fisher was born June 30, 1854, in Jackson, Mississippi, one of seven children. His father, E.S. Fisher, was at the time a sitting judge on the Supreme Court of Mississippi. Shortly after Fisher's birth, the family moved to Grenada, Mississippi. At age eighteen he moved to Georgetown, Texas, and there read law for two years under his elder brother, A.S. Fisher, who had moved earlier to Texas and who would serve in 1915-16 as the first judge of the Criminal and District Court for Travis and Williamson Counties.

Admitted to the Texas bar in 1874, Fisher began his law practice in San Saba. In 1877 he returned to Georgetown where he practiced law with his brother, A.S. Fisher, and John C. Townes. In 1885 he moved to San Angelo.

In 1891 the legislature enlarged the Commission of Appeals, a tribunal to assist the Texas Supreme Court, and Governor James S. Hogg appointed Justice Fisher to one of the new positions. In May 1891 he began service on the commission.

Shortly afterwards, in September 1892, Governor Hogg appointed Justice Fisher Chief Justice of the new Court of Civil Appeals at Austin, which the legislature had authorized in a special session held in 1892. Chief Justice Fisher took the oath of office September 5, 1892, and began service on the court along with Associate Justices William E. Collard and William Mercer Key. The three justices were required to seek election, for staggered terms, in the general election that followed almost immediately on November 8, 1892. They drew lots for terms of two, four, and six years. Chief Justice Fisher was elected to the two-year term, re-elected in 1895, and served thereafter until his death February 10, 1910, of a stroke at age fifty-five.

Chief Justice Fisher was married to Priscilla Pool in San Saba September 15, 1874. They had two children, Della Fisher Harrison and H.C. Fisher, Jr., a lawyer who died of tuberculosis at the age of thirty-five.

William E. Collard

Robertson County

1892-1902

William E. Collard

A son of Reverend James H. and Julia Robinson Collard, William E. Collard was born October 3, 1839, in Conroe, Montgomery County, Texas. He was one of eleven children. His father, a Methodist minister, followed a brother to Texas in 1832 and served in the Army of the Republic. His grandfather, Elijah Collard, followed his sons to Texas in 1833 and was elected to the Consultation of San Felipe in 1835 and served on the General Council, which served briefly as a provisional government for Texas in 1835-36; he later served on the board of land commissioners for Montgomery County in 1837.

William Collard was educated at McKenzie College, a Methodist institution near Clarksville, Red River County, then served in the Civil War. He enlisted in the Tenth Texas Infantry, but by his request was transferred to the Fifteenth Texas Infantry and served in Company B.

In 1865 Collard was admitted to the Texas bar and practiced law in Robertson County from 1865 until 1880 when he was elected district judge. He served until 1887 when Governor Lawrence Sullivan Ross appointed him to the Commission of Appeals.

In 1892 Governor James S. Hogg appointed Justice Collard to the new Court of Civil Appeals at Austin. Justice Collard drew a six-year term and won election to the court in November 1892, where he served until his death in 1902.

Justice Collard was a Knight Templar Mason. In 1865 he married Mattie Glaize, who died in 1867. He married M.E. Heth in September 1868 and they had two sons and a daughter.

William Mercer Key

Williamson County

1892-1923

William Mercer Key

William Mercer Key was born October 20, 1850, in Oglethorpe County, Georgia, to Jasper Newton and Mary Howard Key. His father, a Baptist minister and farmer, came to Gonzales County, Texas, in 1853 with his family and served in Colonel Cook's artillery regiment during the Civil War. The family then settled in Burleson County and later moved to Williamson County.

Key did not attend public schools, but was mostly self-taught while working at the family farm. He remained at home until the death of his mother in 1867, clerked in stores for two or three years, became a merchant on his own, and subsequently moved to Austin to read law in the office of John F. Jones.

Admitted to the Texas bar in 1875, Key moved to Georgetown where he was associated with attorney Thomas Hughes. He served as county attorney, in 1885 became county judge, and in 1888 was appointed and then elected judge of the 26th District Court that served both Williamson and Travis Counties.

When the Court of Civil Appeals at Austin was established in 1892, Governor James S. Hogg appointed Key as an associate justice on the court. Having drawn a four-year term, he was elected to the court in November 1892 and again in 1897, 1903 and 1909. In 1910 Governor Thomas Campbell appointed him to succeed H.C. Fisher as chief justice after Fisher's death. Key remained on the court until his death on November 13, 1923, having served for over thirty-one years—longer than any other justice on the court.

Chief Justice Key was a Mason and a member of the Methodist Episcopal Church, South. He married Izora Scott of Georgetown in December 1876 and they had four children: Walter Scott Key, Mary Key Whitis, Howard W. Key, and Dr. Samuel N. Key.

Sam Streetman

Milam County

1902-1904

Sam Streetman

Sam Streetman was born January 14, 1870, in Cameron, Milam County, Texas. His father, William Bartlett Streetman, was a Cameron merchant and teacher who came to Texas from Georgia in 1852. His mother, Louisa Green, was a native Texan whose father, George Green, moved to Texas in 1836 and served as a private in the Texian Army at the Battle of San Jacinto.

Educated in the public schools at Cameron, Streetman was graduated in 1888 from Southwestern University in Georgetown with a master's degree. He read law in the Cameron office of Judge T.S. Henderson and was admitted to the Texas bar in April 1889. He practiced law with Henderson for the next thirteen years except for a two-year term as county judge of Milam County (1894-96).

In April 1902 Governor Joseph D. Sayers appointed Streetman to the Court of Civil Appeals at Austin to fill the vacancy left by the death of Justice Collard. He won election to a six-year term in November 1902, but retired from the court two years later to practice law in Houston as a partner in the firm of Andrews, Ball and Streetman, now Andrews & Kurth.

During his practice of law in Houston, Justice Streetman was twice president of the Houston Bar Association. Active in many civic clubs and organizations, he was a Mason, a Shriner, an elder in the Presbyterian Church, and a member of the Board of Directors of the National Bank of Commerce and Bankers Mortgage Company. Streetman, Texas, established in 1905 as a station on the Trinity and Brazos Valley (later the Burlington Rock Island) Railroad, was named for Justice Streetman.

In 1923 Justice Streetman and a group of other prominent Houston attorneys founded South Texas Law School, now South Texas College of Law. He served on the board of governors, as a member of the faculty, and was dean of the college from 1931 until his death on November 7, 1933, at age sixty-three.

On December 8, 1892, Justice Streetman married Flora McIver of Cameron. They had six children: Nell Streetman Clarke; Sam, Jr.; Estelle Streetman Lindsey; William McIver, an attorney; Flora Streetman Lawhon; and Charles, who died of diptheria at age two.

James Allen Eidson

Hamilton County

1904-1907

James Allen Eidson

Born April 29, 1848, in Edgefield County, South Carolina, James Allen Eidson was one of six children born to Russell and Caroline Bouknight Eidson, owners of a large plantation. At age sixteen he served a year in the Civil War and, in Charleston at the end of the war, was a second lieutenant in Captain Yancy Dean's Company of South Carolina State Troops.

Eidson attended private schools in South Carolina and was graduated from Wofford College in Spartanburg, South Carolina. He taught school for a year and also read law during that time. Admitted to the South Carolina bar in 1870, he moved to Hamilton County, Texas, and taught school for a year in a country school north of McKinney, Collin County, Texas, before he was admitted to the Texas bar in 1871. He practiced law in Hamilton County for twenty-three years, ten of them in partnership with his son Arthur.

In April 1904 Governor Samuel Willis Tucker Lanham appointed Eidson to the Court of Civil Appeals at Austin to succeed Justice Streetman who had resigned from the court to enter private practice in Houston. Justice Eidson was elected to a six-year term in the next general election, but was forced to retire for health reasons in October 1907. He returned to Hamilton County where he died February 8, 1908.

Justice Eidson married Charity Elizabeth Rice of Hamilton County on August 11, 1874. They had eight children, one of whom died of typhoid fever at age fifteen. Two sons, Arthur Richelieu and Joseph Harvey, practiced law together in Hamilton County and both held public office. Arthur served as county attorney and district attorney and Joseph served as county judge, district attorney, and district judge; his son Joseph, Jr., was a district judge in Fort Worth.

photo by Christianson-Leberman

Benjamin Herbert Rice

Falls County

1907-1918

Benjamin Herbert Rice

The oldest son and first child of Dr. U.A. and Mary Josephine Buckner Rice, Benjamin Herbert Rice was born December 6, 1851, on Woodlawn Plantation, Beaufort District, South Carolina. His paternal great-grandfather fought in the American Revolution in the South Carolina Militia and with Francis Marion, the "Swamp Fox." Dr. Rice was attached to the Army of Northern Virginia during the Civil War and formed the Slappy Guards of Georgia.

Following the death of their mother, Benjamin Rice and his brother and sister were reared in Twiggs County, Georgia. Rice was graduated from the University of Virginia in 1869 and later transferred to a business college where he prepared himself to accept a position in 1872 in Marlin, Falls County, Texas. He later attended the law school at Cumberland University in Lebanon, Tennessee, was graduated in 1877, and was admitted to the Texas bar that summer upon his return to Marlin to practice law in the firm of Martin and Rice. For many years he served on the Marlin School Board and on the Board of Stewards of the Methodist Church.

Rice served as county attorney for Falls County five consecutive terms (1878-85), and then resumed general practice. In 1896 he served one term as county judge of Falls County and again returned to private practice with the firm of Rice and Bartlett. Governor Thomas Campbell appointed him in 1907 to the Court of Civil Appeals at Austin. He took the place of Justice Eidson, who retired due to ill health, and remained on the bench for eleven years. He resigned a few days before his death on November 18, 1918.

Justice Rice married Mary Bowles Carter of Marlin on April 6, 1887. They had nine children, five daughters and four sons, one of whom died in infancy. Their oldest son, Ben H. Rice, Jr., was Chief Justice of the Tenth Court of Civil Appeals at Waco (1941-45) and was a U.S. District Judge for the Western District (1945-74). Four children survive in 1992: Emily Rice Finch, 94; James William Rice, 91; Mary Carter Rice, 89; and Elizabeth Rice Finks, 87.

Charles H. Jenkins

Brown County

1910-1923

Charles H. Jenkins

Charles H. Jenkins was born May 17, 1852, in Dallas County, the son of Jonathan E. and Mahala Bonner Jenkins. Natives of Alabama, his parents settled in Dallas County in 1851, moved to Parker County where his father worked as a surveyor and rancher, then returned to Dallas County in 1861. Jenkins' father served throughout the Civil War, but returned home in broken health and died shortly thereafter.

Jenkins attended private school conducted by the Reverend Mr. Charles Carlton in Dallas, then at age fourteen was sent to Cedar Springs, Falls County, to learn surveying. He became interested in the law, and at age nineteen began to read law in the offices of Kendall and Ault in Dallas. His studies were interrupted in 1871 when he was placed in charge of the surveyor's office in Dallas County, and in 1873 he was appointed city engineer of the city of Dallas. He kept up his law studies, however, and in March 1874 was admitted to the Texas bar.

Jenkins practiced law for five years in Dallas before moving about 1880 to Brownwood, Brown County, then a frontier town about to become a point on the railroad. He served as an alderman, one term as mayor, and was on the school board for twenty-six consecutive years, fourteen years as president.

In 1907 Jenkins won election to the Texas Legislature. Re-elected in 1909, he resigned in March 1910 to accept Governor Thomas Campbell's appointment to the Court of Civil Appeals, replacing Justice Key when he was appointed chief justice. The following November Jenkins was elected to the unexpired three years of Justice Key's six-year term, and he served on the court until his resignation in 1923 at the age of seventy-one. In 1924 he served as chairman of the Committee to Codify Texas Laws.

Jenkins was a prominent member of the Odd Fellows fraternity, the Woodmen of the World, an honorary member of the Austin Press Club, and a member of the Texas State Historical Association. He died February 23, 1931, in Brownwood.

In September 1873 Justice Jenkins married Annie E. Smith, a former Dallas classmate. They had three daughters: Willie Jenkins Miller, Annie Jenkins Johnson, and Roberta Jenkins Shropshire.

John W. Brady
Travis County
1918-1923

John W. Brady

Born about 1870 in Austin, Travis County, Texas, John W. Brady was one of five children born to James and Agnes Brady. His father was a grocer, born in Ireland, and his mother was English. Brady received a law degree from the law department of The University of Texas in 1896.

At various points in his career Brady had a law partnership with E.B. Robertson of Fort Worth, was a county attorney for Travis County, and served as an attorney for the State Banking Board and as an assistant attorney general under Jewel P. Lightfoot. He also worked as special counsel for Governor Miriam "Ma" Ferguson.

In 1918, following the death of Justice Rice, Governor William P. Hobby appointed Justice Brady to the Court of Civil Appeals at Austin. Justice Brady served on the court until 1923 when he was defeated for election by James Blair.

In 1930 Justice Brady was tried in Austin for the murder of a young woman, Lehlia Highsmith, in front of her Austin boarding house on the night of November 9, 1929. She was a stenographer at the Commission of Appeals, a position Judge Brady had helped her obtain. District Attorney Henry Brooks sought the death penalty and was assisted in the prosecution by Roy C. Archer (q.v.). Brady pleaded temporary insanity caused by chronic drinking. The trial ended in a deadlocked jury.

In a second trial, in Dallas County, Justice Brady was found guilty of murder without malice and sentenced to three years in prison. The verdict was upheld by the Court of Criminal Appeals in December 1930. After his release from the penitentiary in Huntsville, Brady returned to Austin and was engaged in legal research until his death December 13, 1943.

Justice Brady married Nell C. Burns on July 18, 1901. She remained at his side through his two trials and lived with him in Austin after his release from prison. They had no children.

photo by Christianson-Leberman

James Wooten McClendon

Travis County

1923-1949

James Wooten McClendon

James Wooten McClendon was born November 1, 1873, in West Point, Georgia, to James Wooten and Annie Eliza Thompson McClendon. His father, a merchant and mayor of West Point, was unable to serve in the Civil War due to poor health, but maintained a private commissary for the benefit of the Confederate government. His father died in 1882. In 1889 his widowed mother and her five children moved to Laredo, Texas, where she worked for twenty-one years as a missionary sponsored by the Women's Board of the Methodist Episcopal Church, South.

In 1895 McClendon was graduated from The University of Texas at Austin, with a bachelor of arts degree, and in 1897 with a bachelor of laws from the law department. While in law school he was an editor on the *Texas Law Review*, a member of the Order of the Coif, and manager of the university's 1896 football team.

Later in life he was an active member of the Texas Alumni Association and served on the ways and means committees that helped build Gregory Gymnasium, Memorial Stadium, Kirby Hall, and the University YMCA. A sixty-year member of the Masons and the Grand Master of Texas in 1931, he was also instrumental in bringing about the construction of the Scottish Rite Dormitory and served for over forty years on its board of directors. He was a contributor to the University Methodist Bible Chair and a life-long member of the Town and Gown Club.

McClendon practiced law in Austin for twenty-one years (1897-1918). During the later years of her life, Elizabet Ney was a client of McClendon's. While in private practice, Justice McClendon served as president of the Travis County Bar Association (1912-13).

In 1918 Governor William P. Hobby appointed McClendon to the Commission of Appeals where he served for five years, the last two years as chief justice. In 1923, upon the death of Justice Key, Governor Pat Neff appointed McClendon Chief Justice of the Court of Civil Appeals at Austin, a post he held until he retired on January 1, 1949, at age seventy-five. In 1934 Justice McClendon ran for the Texas Supreme Court, but was defeated by John Sharp in a run-off in the Democratic primary. When Chief Justice McClendon left the bench, he gave his private law library to The University of Texas Law School.

While on the bench, Chief Justice McClendon was active in both state and national legal organizations. He proposed the statute that created the Texas Judicial Council, and was appointed by the Texas Supreme Court to serve on an advisory committee to revise the rules of civil procedure.

Long active in the Austin community, Chief Justice McClendon was a member of the Austin Heritage Society, on the Board of Stewards of the First Methodist Church, and a charter member of the Texas Fine Arts Association. He was the first president of the association (1911-17) and later served two additional terms. As a member of the association, he was instrumental in establishing the Elizabet Ney Museum and the Laguna Gloria Art Museum, both in Austin, and in 1970, at the age of ninety-six, he established a trust, the Elizabet Ney Texas Fine Arts Association, McClendon Foundation, to benefit the museum. On January 9, 1972, Chief Justice McClendon died in Austin at age ninety-eight.

Chief Justice McClendon married Ann Hale Watt of Waco on December 14, 1904. They had two daughters, Mary Ann McClendon and Elizabeth McClendon Knight. His granddaughter, Rev. Ann Knight Hoey, is married to Texas artist William Hoey.

THE GREAT TRIUMVIRATE
From left to right: Justice Blair; Chief Justice McClendon; Justice Baugh. The three judges served together for twenty-three consecutive years (December 1923-January 1947) and laid the foundation for the state's administrative law.
Photo courtesy of the Austin History Center, Austin Public Library.

photo by Christianson-Leberman

Mallory Benton Blair

Travis County

1923-1947

Mallory Benton Blair

One of three children born to James Benton and Sarah Reed Blair, Mallory Benton Blair was born September 11, 1887, on a farm near Killeen, Bell County, Texas. When Blair's mother died, his father married Jennie Lena Harkins and they had seven children. James was sheriff of Bell County in the early 1900s and for a time he and his family lived over the county jail.

Attending private school in Belton and graduating with honors from Wedemeyer Academy (later Belton Academy) in 1909, Blair worked his way through school by selling horses, cattle, and other livestock. He taught eighth grade at the academy for two years before graduating in 1912 from the law department of The University of Texas.

Blair practiced law in Belton after law school, and in 1916 was elected county judge, a position he held for four years. In 1921 he was elected for a two-year term as judge of the 27th Judicial District Court serving Bell, Lampasas and Mills counties. In 1923 he was elected to the Court of Civil Appeals at Austin on which he sat for twenty-four years.

Justice Blair was defeated for re-election in 1947 and returned to private practice, in partnership with Gibson Randle and Gaynor Kendall. His practice was interrupted in mid-1947, however, when President Truman appointed Blair to serve on the American Military Tribunal III at Nuremberg, Germany, a body charged to try war crimes committed during the World War II period. After nearly a year on the tribunal, he returned to his Austin law practice.

Governor Price Daniel appointed Justice Blair as chairman of the Commission on the Study of Industrial and Occupational Safety. He was also a member of the State Board of Law Examiners from 1953 until shortly before his death on March 15, 1962, at age seventy-five.

Justice Blair, an active member of the First Methodist Church in Austin, was on the Board of Stewards and taught a men's Bible class there for fifteen years.

On May 28, 1913, Justice Blair married Margaret (Maggie) Dougherty of Burnet. They are survived by two daughters, Sarah Blair Dougherty and Dawn Blair Woodward.

James Harvey Baugh

Brown County

1923-1947

James Harvey Baugh

Born March 11, 1884, on a ranch near Brownwood, Brown County, Texas, James Harvey Baugh was one of eleven children born to Washington Morgan and Canzada Burnett Baugh. They came to Texas from Georgia about 1850 and first settled in Kaufman County. His father "Morg," a rancher and farmer, moved his family to Brown County in 1854.

Baugh was educated in a nearby rural school and in Brownwood. In 1904 he was graduated from Howard Payne College, Brownwood, from Baylor University in 1906, and studied law for one year at Brown University, Providence, Rhode Island, in 1907. He taught at Howard Payne College for a year before entering law school, and in 1922 was awarded an honorary Doctor of Laws Degree from the college. Baugh was graduated from the law department of The University of Texas in 1911, admitted to the Texas bar the same year, and practiced briefly in Brownwood, then in Ballinger, Runnells County. He was elected to the Texas Senate in 1921 and held office until Governor Pat Neff appointed him to the Court of Civil Appeals at Austin on August 1, 1923, following Justice Jenkins' resignation.

Justice Baugh also enjoyed a military career that spanned twenty-seven years. He was graduated from the First Officers Training Camp, Leon Springs, Texas, in 1917, and during World War I he served in the Judge Advocate General's Department. Having obtained the rank of major at the end of World War I, he remained in the army reserve and took an active part in bringing the Reserve Officer Training Corps to The University of Texas at Austin. He was ordered again to active duty in 1941 at the beginning of World War II, at the age of fifty-seven. Taking a two-year leave of absence from the court, he served as Staff Judge Advocate General, San Antonio Air Service Command, Kelly Field, Texas. He returned to the Army Reserve and in 1944 retired as a colonel.

Active in the Baptist Church, Justice Blair was also a Mason and served as president of the Austin Lions Club in 1932-33.

Justice Baugh died in office November 24, 1947, at age sixty-three. He had married Rosa Moffett of Dilley, Texas, on December 2, 1917. They did not have any children.

photo by Christianson-Leberman

Robert G. Hughes

Tom Green County

1947-1971

Robert G. Hughes

Born in New York City November 22, 1899, Robert G. Hughes was the son of Reverend William and Jennie Godber Hughes. His father was a Presbyterian minister who was born in Ireland and came to America at the age of twenty-six. His mother was from Waco and the family moved to Hico, Hamilton County, Texas, when Hughes was an infant.

From age twelve, Hughes worked at odd jobs to finance his education. After graduating from Hico High School, he served in the navy during World War I. After the war he enrolled in The University of Texas from which he received a bachelor of laws in June 1926. He was admitted to the bar that same year.

After receiving his law license, Hughes moved to San Angelo, Tom Green County, where he practiced law for twenty years. While in private practice, he also served as city attorney of San Angelo 1928-36 and district attorney of the 51st Judicial District 1943-46.

In 1947 Hughes defeated Justice Blair, a four-term incumbent on the Court of Civil Appeals at Austin. Hughes later ran unsuccessfully for associate justice of the Supreme Court of Texas in 1957 and for chief justice of that court in 1961.

Justice Hughes retired from the Court of Civil Appeals at Austin in 1971 at age seventy-one. He moved from Austin to Houston where he died August 10, 1981. He had married Elva Ann Sheffield of Grand Saline, Texas, on June 16, 1927. They are survived by four children: Robert G., Jr., Elizabeth Hughes Fosberg, Nancy Hughes Bell, and Jerry Lee.

F. Raymond Gray

San Saba County

1947-1961

F. Raymond Gray

F. Raymond Gray was born January 9, 1891, in Cherokee, San Saba County, Texas, one of twelve children born to George J. and Tilitha Williams Gray. Gray's father, a rancher who came to Texas in 1856 and settled in San Saba County in 1860, lived to be ninety-eight years of age and served with his three brothers in the Civil War. Reuben, one of the brothers, was a captain in the Texas Rangers charged with protecting the frontier from Indians during the war.

Gray attended public schools in San Saba County, then The University of Texas at Austin where he received a bachelor of laws in 1915. He was admitted to the Texas bar that same year and returned to San Saba to enter private practice. He served as county attorney 1926-32 and as judge of the 33d District Court 1936-47.

Governor Beauford Jester appointed Gray to the Court of Civil Appeals at Austin on November 27, 1947, to succeed Justice Baugh who had died in office. Justice Gray served on the court for fourteen years before his retirement October 1, 1961. Returning to the ranch in Cherokee that his father had established before the Civil War, Justice Gray pursued his interest in ranching and hunting before his death twelve years later on August 3, 1973 at age eighty-two.

Justice Gray was active in the Methodist Church and in the affairs of the American Legion and the State Bar of Texas. He served 1946-47 as chairman of the Judicial Section of the State Bar.

On September 11, 1935, Justice Gray married Gertrude Foster of Georgetown. They are survived by their three children, Elizabeth Gray Johnson, Lester Gray, and George Gray.

photo by Christianson-Leberman

Roy Colman Archer

Travis County

1949-1967

Roy Colman Archer

Roy Colman Archer was born July 12, 1890, near Evant in Coryell County, Texas. He was one of ten children born to John McQuatty and Melissa Mullins Archer. His father, married twice, had twenty-one children and was a farmer and rancher who had come to Texas in the early 1840s. When Roy Archer was nine, his family moved to the Panhandle where he attended Goodnight Academy and Ford's Academy. In 1914 he was graduated from The University of Texas at Austin, and was admitted to the Texas bar. He published *The Buda Star*, in Buda, Hays County, Texas, that same year.

Roy's first public service was as United States Commissioner for the Slavic States from 1918-21, and on January 2, 1920, he became U.S. Commissioner for the Western District of Texas.

During the early 1920s, Archer practiced law in Austin with James R. Hamilton, Jr. In 1926 he was elected county attorney of Travis County and in 1930 county judge, serving one term before returning to private practice with Marion Fowler. In 1937 Archer was elected judge of the 126th Judicial District Court in Austin, and served twelve years in that position before his election as chief justice in 1949 to the Court of Civil Appeals at Austin. He served eighteen years on the court before his retirement in 1967 at age seventy-six.

Archer was president of the Travis County Bar Association in 1939 and for many years was chairman of the Travis County Juvenile Board. He also served many years on the Federal Land Bank Board. He was a fifty-year Mason and a member of Central Christian Church where he taught a Bible class for over forty years. He owned and supervised a working farm at Creedmore, Travis County, Texas, until his death in Austin October 29, 1973.

Chief Justice Archer married Kate Cocke of San Antonio on Christmas Day, 1910. Her father established Cocke and Denman, the oldest law firm in San Antonio. Their twin boys died in infancy and their remaining son, Branch Leroy, was killed at age twenty-one in a hunting accident. Their three daughters are Catherine Archer Tyson, Maude Archer Ellis, and Helen Archer Brown. After his wife died in 1956, Justice Archer married Helen Woodman on July 16, 1960, and she lives in Austin.

photo by Christianson-Leberman

C. K. Richards

Travis County

1961-1963

C. K. Richards

Born in Trenton, New Jersey, June 9, 1891, C.K. "Cap" Richards was the only child of Howard Newton Richards, a pharmacist, and Lillian Kelly Richards. C.K. attended Brown University, Providence, Rhode Island, 1907-9, and received a bachelor of laws in 1912 from the University of Virginia. Admitted to the Missouri bar in 1913, he practiced law in Kansas City, Missouri, 1913-25, and served in World War I as an officer in the Adjutant General's Department.

Admitted to the Texas bar in 1925, Richards practiced in Brownsville for seventeen years, from 1925 to 1942. He was associated with the law firm founded by Judge James B. Wells, and was later a partner with J.K. Wells, Judge Well's son.

After service during World War II as a captain in the military police, Richards moved to Austin in 1944 where he served as an assistant attorney general under Grover Sellers and Price Daniel until 1953. In 1953-55 he was special assistant to the U.S. Attorney General during the Eisenhower administration. He returned to the Texas Attorney General's Office in 1957 where he served under Will Wilson until 1961.

In November 1961 Governor Price Daniel appointed Richards to the Court of Civil Appeals at Austin to fill Justice Gray's unexpired term following his resignation. Justice Richards did not seek election to the court at the end of his term on January 1, 1963, but returned to private practice. He died on November 19, 1965, at the age of seventy-five. He and his wife, who died in August 1980, both donated their bodies to The University of Texas Medical Branch in Galveston.

Justice Richards married Dorothy Wilson of San Angelo on November 1, 1932. They have one son, Howard N. Richards, a lawyer in Austin.

photo courtesy of Center for Legal History, State Bar of Texas

John C. Phillips

Travis County

1963-1985

John C. Phillips

John C. Phillips was born November 24, 1917, in San Antonio, Bexar County, Texas, a twelfth-generation descendant of the Canary Islanders who founded the city and a direct descendant of its first mayor, Juan Leal Goraz, and a later mayor, Joseph Dwyer. His father, Hiram Alfred Phillips, was a surgeon and chief of staff of the Santa Rosa Hospital in San Antonio, and his mother was Annette Dwyer Schmitt of San Antonio. Phillips has a brother, Nash Phillips, and a sister, Annette Phillips Sadler.

Phillips was graduated in 1935 from the Texas Military Institute in San Antonio, and in 1941 from The University of Texas at Austin, with a bachelor of arts and a bachelor of laws. He had just resigned his commission in the army, to join the Federal Bureau of Investigation, when the Japanese bombed Pearl Harbor. He spent the remaining war years as a special agent of the Bureau and its Secret Intelligence Service.

After the war Phillips for a year was law clerk for Supreme Court of Texas Judges Taylor, Smedley, Slatton and Hart. During 1947-49 he was a hearings examiner for the Texas Railroad Commission in its Gas Utilities and Oil and Gas Divisions and afterwards was a sole practitioner for eleven years. He served as an assistant attorney general under Will Wilson.

In 1963 Phillips was elected associate justice of the Court of Civil Appeals at Austin, and four years later was elected chief justice. He served twenty-two years on the court.

A former member the Texas Law Review Board of Directors, Chief Justice Phillips is a Fellow of the Texas Bar Foundation.

Chief Justice Phillips is married to Peggy Smith of Minneapolis, Minnesota, and they have three sons, John C., James Chrisman, and William Taylor (all lawyers), and a daughter, Peggy Phillips Singleton.

photo by Christianson-Leberman

Trueman Edgar O'Quinn

Travis County

1967-1980

Trueman Edgar O'Quinn

Born in Vernon Parrish, Louisiana, May 7, 1905, Trueman Edgar O'Quinn was one of three children of Dallas Patrick and Florence Isabelle O'Conner O'Quinn. The O'Quinns moved in 1917 to East Texas.

An Eagle Scout, Trueman attended Beaumont High School before enrolling in The University of Texas in 1922. By the time he received his bachelor of laws in 1932, he had supported himself as a writer of nationally syndicated news stories, taught fencing, served as editor of the *Daily Texan* (the university newspaper), and won election to the Texas Legislature where he served 1930-31.

Following his graduation from law school, Trueman was in private practice in Austin until his appointment as assistant city attorney in 1936 and as city attorney in 1938, a position he held until 1950 except for four years in the army during World War II.

During the war, O'Quinn was Staff Judge Advocate of the 101st Airborne Division, supervised court-martial trials in Normandy after the invasion, fought in four major battles, served with the army of occupation in Germany, and supervised the out processing of 90,000 German prisoners in Austria.

Returning to Austin in 1946, O'Quinn resumed service as city attorney until 1950 when he returned to private practice. During this time he also served as Travis County Democratic Chairman for fourteen years and worked for two years as legal counsel for The University of Texas at Austin. In 1967 Governor John Connally appointed him to the Court of Civil Appeals at Austin to serve the unexpired term of Judge Phillips who was elected chief justice in 1967. Justice O'Quinn served on the court for thirteen years before his retirement in January 1980. He died January 4, 1990.

Long active in civic and legal affairs, Justice O'Quinn amassed a collection of O. Henry first editions, magazines, photographs, manuscripts and furniture associated with the famous author, all of which he gave in 1983 to the Austin History Center. He was co-author with Dr. Jenny Lind Porter of *Time to Write: How William Sidney Porter became O. Henry.*

Justice O'Quinn married Hazel Hedick of Austin on November 26, 1929. They are survived by their two sons, Kerry and Trueman, Jr.

photo by Allen Photography

Bob Eric Shannon

Travis County

1971-1991

Bob Eric Shannon

Bob Eric Shannon was born in Brown County, Texas, December 29, 1933, to John Edward and Nora Elizabeth Shannon, and reared on the family farm with his three brothers, John, Charley and Kent.

Bob was graduated as valedictorian from Early High School in 1951, then from The University of Texas at Austin with a bachelor of arts. He was a member of the Silver Spurs, a men's honorary service organization. In 1957 he was graduated from The University of Texas School of Law, where he served on the editorial board of the *Texas Law Review* and was a member of Phi Delta Phi, an honorary legal fraternity.

Following six months in the army, Shannon joined the Houston law firm of Fulbright, Crooker, Freeman, Bates and Jaworski. A year later he returned to Austin where he served as assistant attorney general in the administration of Will Wilson. Afterwards, he entered private law practice with James R. Meyers in the Austin law office of Coleman Gay. Bob later formed a law partnership with Meyers and Bob Landis Armstrong until Meyers was elected to the district bench in 1965. Bob then became a partner in Small, Herring, Craig, Werkenthin and Shannon where he remained until his election in 1971 to the Court of Civil Appeals at Austin as associate justice.

Shannon was named Outstanding Young Lawyer of Travis County in 1970, and served several terms as president of the Heritage Society of Austin.

Justice Shannon served on the court for twenty years, the last six as chief justice. In January 1991, on his retirement from the court, he joined the Austin office of the law firm of Baker-Botts.

Chief Justice Shannon is married to the former Camille Newberry of Austin. They have two daughters, Laurel Shannon and Elizabeth Camille Shannon Hudson. Another daughter, Lesley Brevard Shannon, died in 1989.

Robert O. Smith

Travis County

1980-1981

Robert O. Smith

Born September 21, 1922, in Running Water, Brown County, Texas, Robert O. "Bob" Smith was the son of Clyde and Ruby Smith. He was reared on the family farm in Brown County.

After graduation in 1940 from Rising Star High School, Bob served in the Army Air Corps during World War II and was decorated for valor. During college he served in the United States Air Force Reserve and was briefly called to active duty during the Korean War.

Bob was graduated from The University of Texas with a bachelor of business administration and from The University of Texas School of Law with a bachelor of laws. Immediately upon graduation he joined the district attorney's office in Travis County and served as first assistant district attorney from 1956-60. In 1960 Smith joined the attorney general's office under Will Wilson.

In private practice from 1964 to 1967 with John Allen and Price Ashton, Smith was appointed in March 1967 to serve as county attorney for Travis County. In October 1969 Governor Preston Smith appointed him interim district attorney. Smith won election to two terms as district attorney, and during those years he served as the lead prosecutor in several famous cases involving state officials.

Smith was president of the Texas District and County Attorney's Association in 1973, and served two terms as chairman of the State Bar Committee on the Penal Code 1975-77. He helped establish the Austin Rape Crisis Center and was recognized by three citizens groups for his service to the community and to law enforcement.

In 1977 Smith returned to private practice and was a partner in the law firm of Salmanson, Smith & Mouer. Governor William Clements appointed him in March 1980 to the Court of Civil Appeals at Austin to succeed Justice O'Quinn who had retired. Justice Smith was the first Republican ever to serve on the court, but he was defeated in the 1980 general election and returned to private practice. He remained in private practice until his death on September 24, 1990.

Justice Smith was married to Betty Thompson and they have a son, Robert Conrad. His first wife died in 1964, and he married Joan Lynn Porter of Austin. They have two daughters, Jane Smith Howard and Sally Jean Smith.

photo by Christianson-Leberman

John E. Powers

Travis County

1981-

John E. Powers

A fifth-generation Texan, John E. Powers was born December 23, 1935, in Fort Worth, Texas. His father was Elmer Powers, a baker, and his mother was Inez Corder Powers, both born and reared in Thurber, Erath County, Texas. His brother is Norman Powers; his sister, Sybil Powers Cooley, died in 1988.

Powers attended public school in Fort Worth until 1950 when his family moved to Lubbock. After graduation from Lubbock High School in 1954, he attended Texas Technological College for one year before transferring to The University of Texas at Austin. He served in the army 1958-60, then returned to the university and received a bachelor of business administration in 1961. Recalled to active duty for the Berlin Crisis in 1961, he served another year of active duty before returning to Austin in 1962. He worked two years as an auditor for the Texas Highway Department before enrolling in The University of Texas School of Law in 1965.

After graduation from law school in 1968, Powers practiced law in Austin for twelve years, ten of them in partnership with William S. Rose. In 1981 he won election to the Court of Civil Appeals at Austin.

Justice Powers is a Fellow of the Texas Bar Foundation and a member of the Council of the Administrative and Public Law Section of the State Bar. He was chairman of the Council during 1990-91. He is the author of a book on Texas administrative law entitled *Agency Adjudication* and two law review articles, "Judicial Review of the Findings of Fact Made by Texas Administrative Agencies in Contested Cases," in the *Texas Tech Law Review*, and "Fact Finding in the Courts of Military Review," in the *Baylor Law Review*. He presently serves as a consultant to Bancroft-Whitney Publishing Company in its revision of Roy McDonald's *Texas Civil Practice*.

A member of the naval reserve for twenty-three years, Justice Powers holds the rank of captain and is a senior commissioner on the Navy-Marine Corps Court of Military Review in Washington, D.C.

He is married to Deborah Daniels Powers of San Antonio. They have two daughters, Ann and Catherine.

photo by Wallace Studio

Earl Wesley Smith

Tom Green County

1982-1986

Earl Wesley Smith

One of seven children, Earl Wesley Smith was born November 6, 1919, on a farm in Hale County, Texas, to James William and Sallie Elizabeth Baskin Smith.

After graduating from Plainview High School, Smith was graduated as valedictorian from Schreiner Institute, Kerrville, Texas, and attended The University of Texas at Austin. He served with the Army Air Corps in Panama during World War II and was graduated in 1947 from The University of Texas School of Law. During law school Smith served as a quiz master and was a member of Phi Tau Kappa, an honorary law fraternity.

Smith practiced law in San Angelo for twenty-five years, including service as city attorney (1950-51), county attorney (1951-52), and district attorney (1952-53). During this period he was president of the Tom Green County Bar Association (1951), served on State bar committees to revise the penal code and the code of criminal procedure, and was appointed to two state commissions. Smith served two terms on the executive committee of the Democratic Party of Texas and two terms on the board of the San Angelo Independent School District.

Smith won election in 1972 to the 51st Judicial District Court in San Angelo where he served for ten years. Governor William P. Clements appointed Judge Smith to the Court of Appeals at Austin in September 1982, and Smith was elected to the court in 1983. Justice Smith served on the court until his retirement in 1986. He continues to serve as a senior judge in Austin district courts and on the Court of Appeals at Austin.

A charter member of the Texas Bar Foundation, Justice Smith is also a former faculty member of the Texas College of the Judiciary (1976-84). He is a past president of the West Texas Christian Foundation and an elder in the Church of Christ.

Justice Smith has been married to Mozelle Owens of San Angelo since August 31, 1941. They have three children: Robert Earl Smith and Janice Kay Smith Moss, both lawyers, and Martha Nell Smith, Ph.D.

Robert A. Gammage

Travis County

1982-1991

Robert A. Gammage

Robert A. "Bob" Gammage was born March 13, 1938, in Houston, Harris County, Texas, the second of three children born to Paul and Sara Ella Marshall Gammage. Although licensed to practice law, his father was a salesman, and his mother worked in public school administration. Gammage's maternal ancestors migrated to Texas in 1821 from Maryland and Kentucky and took part in the Texas Revolution; his father's family moved to Texas from Georgia in 1887. His great-great grandfather, Travis S. Cochran, served in the 21st State Legislature (1889-91) from Polk and San Jacinto Counties.

Graduated in 1956 from Milby High School in Houston, Gammage received an associate degree from Del Mar College, a bachelor's degree from the University of Corpus Christi, and a master's degree from Sam Houston State University. He was graduated in 1969 from The University of Texas School of Law and has a master of laws in judicial process from the University of Virginia School of Law.

Gammage served in 1959-60 on active duty in the army and is currently a captain in the naval reserve.

Engaged in private practice in both Houston and Austin, Gammage also served in the Texas House of Representatives (1971-73), the Texas Senate (1973-76), the United States Congress (1977-79), and was an assistant attorney general under Mark White (1979-80). Governor William P. Clements appointed Gammage to the Court of Appeals at Austin in September 1982 and Gammage won election to the court in 1983. He served on the court until his election to the Supreme Court in Texas in 1991.

While on the Court of Appeals at Austin, Justice Gammage was a delegate to the first Governor's Conference on the Judiciary and served on the Texas Judicial Council. He was vice-chairman of the State Bar Committee on Funding for the Judicial Branch of Government and currently chairs the Texas Judicial Education Executive Committee.

Justice Gammage is married to Lynda Ray Hallmark, a native of Llano. They have one son, Samuel Paul Gammage. Justice Gammage's three children by a previous marriage are daughters Terry Lynne and Sara Noel Gammage Newman, and son Robert, Jr.

James C. Brady

Travis County

1982-1988

James C. Brady

The eldest son of Neal and Mabel Brady, James C. "Jim" Brady was born September 3, 1919, in Des Moines, Iowa, where his parents were pharmacists and owners of a drugstore.

Brady attended public and parochial schools in Des Moines, and his debating skills earned him a scholarship to Grinnell College in Iowa. He attended the University of Iowa and was graduated from the Drake University Law School in 1942, then practiced law for two years in Des Moines before entering the army to serve in World War II. He served at the Army War College, at the Pentagon, and as a military intelligence (CIC) officer at Fort Sam Houston, Texas.

After passing the Texas bar in 1946, Brady went to work as an assistant district attorney for Bexar County. In 1949 he entered private practice in San Antonio, and later practiced law in Houston until 1979 when he moved to Austin.

In September 1982 Governor William P. Clements appointed Brady to the Court of Appeals at Austin, and Brady won election to the court in 1983. While on the court, Justice Brady published an article in the *Texas Tech Law Review,* "Reducing Appellate Delay—a 'Fast Track' System," and an article in the *Texas Bar Journal,* "The Kentucky Video Experience: An Example of Judicial Economy." Defeated for re-election in 1989, he resigned from the court in September 1988 to enter private practice.

Justice Brady served as president of the San Antonio Young Lawyers Association (1952) and vice-president of the Texas Young Lawyers Association (1953). He is a former chief justice of the national legal fraternity Delta Theta Phi, a past president of Sierra Club, Austin, a life member of the Texas Lions League for Crippled Children, and a member of the American Judicature Society. In 1988 Justice Brady chaired the State Bar Committee to Aid Local Bar Associations.

Justice Brady is married to the former Shari Shurmon of San Antonio. They have four children: Teresa, Bridget, Jimmy, and Shari Ann.

photo by John Jefferson

James Lee Carroll

Bell County

1985-

James Lee Carroll

Born January 22, 1948, to Joe and Marjorie Carroll, James "Jimmy" Lee Carroll was born in Temple, Bell County, Texas. His father was an attorney who served as city attorney and school-board attorney for the Temple schools. Justice Carroll's brother Joe is judge of the 27th Judicial District Court in Temple and a former district attorney. Their sister, Marjo Carroll, lives in Austin.

Carroll was graduated from Temple High School in 1966 and received both his undergraduate and law degrees from The University of Texas at Austin. In law school he was a member of Phi Delta Phi honorary legal fraternity.

Following graduation from law school, Carroll served for a year as Assistant Director of the Elections Division under Secretary of State Mark White. He then returned to Temple and entered private law practice with his brother. During this time he also served as president of the Texas Bank in Temple.

In 1985 Governor Mark White appointed Carroll to the Court of Appeals at Austin to fill Justice Bob Shannon's seat when he became chief justice. When Chief Justice Bob Shannon retired in 1991, Justice Carroll was elected chief justice.

Chief Justice Carroll is active in numerous civic and community activities, and he and his family attend the First United Methodist Church in Temple. He is a former chairman of the Texas Council of Justices, the statewide association of all courts of appeals justices, and a Fellow of the Texas Bar Foundation. In 1992 he received a citation from the president of the State Bar of Texas for his service to the state bar.

Chief Justice Carroll is married to Madelon Elaine Mitchell of San Antonio. They have two sons, Mitchell and Marshall.

photo by Jim Bean

Marilyn Aboussie

Tom Green County

1986-

Marilyn Aboussie

Born in Wichita Falls, Wichita County, Texas, Marilyn Aboussie was born June 9, 1948, to Marjorie and Eddie J. Aboussie. She has a sister, Carol Aboussie Burnam, and two brothers, Joey Aboussie and Dr. Kenneth Aboussie. They are the grandchildren of four Lebanese immigrants who settled in Texas and Oklahoma in the early 1900s.

After graduation from Wichita Falls High School, Marilyn earned a degree in the Honors Program in 1969 from Midwestern University. After working two years in Washington, D.C., she entered The University of Texas School of Law and also served as a legislative aide to State Representative Dave Allred of Wichita Falls.

After graduation from law school in 1974, Aboussie became an associate in the Houston law firm of Foreman, Dyess, Prewett, Rosenberg and Henderson. In 1976 she and her husband moved to San Angelo where both became partners in the law firm of Smith, Davis, Rose, Finley and Hofmann.

In 1983 Governor Mark White appointed Justice Aboussie to the newly created 340th District Court of Tom Green County. She won election to the court in 1984 and chaired the county's juvenile board that established a juvenile justice center for the region. In 1986 she received the Charles O. Betts outstanding juvenile judge award for Texas, and in 1987 she was chosen the outstanding alumna of Midwestern University.

When Justice Earl Smith retired in 1986 from the Court of Appeals at Austin, Governor Mark White appointed Justice Aboussie to the vacancy. She was elected to the court in 1989.

Justice Aboussie is a past president of both the Tom Green County Young Lawyers Association and the Tom Green County Bar Association and a past chairman of the General Practice Section of the State Bar, the first woman to hold each office. She also served as vice-chairman of the State Bar committee that established the Women and the Law Section, and is a Fellow of the Texas Bar Foundation. A member of Leadership Texas, she has also served on many civic and charitable boards .

Justice Aboussie is married to John Alvin Hay, Jr., a certified public accountant and a partner in a San Angelo law firm. They have a son, John Alvin Hay, III.

photo by John Jefferson

J. Woodfin Jones

Travis County

1989-

J. Woodfin Jones

J. Woodfin "Woodie" Jones was born September 26, 1949, in Austin, Travis County, Texas, to Perry and Catherine Jones. His brother Stephen is an attorney and his two sisters are Beverly and Mary Catherine.

Jones comes from a family of Texas lawyers. His father was county attorney for Travis County. His uncle, Herman Jones, was an attorney in Austin and a district judge; his uncle, Harold Jones, was an attorney and a former mayor of Wichita Falls; and yet another uncle, Woodfin Butte, was an attorney and law professor at The University of Texas School of Law. Jones' maternal grandfather, George Butte, was Dean of The University of Texas School of Law before resigning in 1924 to run an unsuccessful gubernatorial campaign against Miriam A. "Ma" Ferguson.

A 1967 graduate of Stephen F. Austin High School in Austin, Jones was graduated Phi Beta Kappa from The University of Texas at Austin, and in 1975 was graduated from The University of Texas School of Law, where he was a director of the Legal Research Board. He served in the Texas Army National Guard at Camp Mabry, Austin, from 1972 to 1978.

Jones worked one year as a law clerk for Chief Justice J. Curtiss Brown, of the Fourteenth Court of Civil Appeals in Houston. He then joined the Houston firm of Bracewell and Patterson, where he practiced for five years. In 1981 he returned to Austin to become a partner in the firm of Sneed, Vine, Wilkerson, Selman and Perry. He was elected in 1989 to the Court of Appeals at Austin.

Jones served as president of the Travis County Bar Association in 1987-88 and is a Fellow of the Texas Bar Foundation. He and his family are active members of the Episcopal Church.

Justice Jones is married to the former Linda Eitelman of Austin. In addition to a daughter from a previous marriage, Monica Rowlett, the Joneses have two children, Jeremy Woodfin and Jennifer Meghan.

photo by John Jefferson

Bea Ann Smith

Travis County

1991-

Bea Ann Smith

Bea Ann Smith was born November 16, 1943, in Ardmore, Oklahoma, the daughter of L.B. Asbury, Jr., and Betty Slocombe Asbury Smith. She is the adopted daughter of Robert Bruce Smith and has two brothers, Bruce Alan Smith and Barry Asher Smith.

Smith moved to Texas at an early age and was graduated in 1961 from Midland High School. At The University of Texas at Austin, she was active in Orange Jackets, the University Y, and the Students' Association. She was named Phi Beta Kappa, Outstanding Student, and a Woodrow Wilson Fellow and was graduated in 1965 with honors in Plan II. She received her master's degree in 1967 from Brandeis University.

After teaching English at Texas Southern University and in various programs abroad and in Texas, Smith enrolled in 1972 at The University of Texas School of Law. She served on the *Texas Law Review* and was graduated with honors in 1975. The following year she served a judicial clerkship with Judge Thomas Gibbs Gee, United States Court of Appeals for the Fifth Circuit.

Smith practiced law in Austin for fifteen years, in her own law offices and with Graves, Dougherty, Hearon & Moody. She also served as an adjunct professor at The University of Texas School of Law. Smith was the founder of Austin Lawyers Care and she helped organize the Travis County Women Lawyers' Association and Women and the Law Section of the State Bar. She has been active in bar association work at the county, state, and national level. Her community activities include the Austin Women's Center, Women and Their Work, the Austin Dispute Resolution Center, the New Texas Festival, and All Saints' Episcopal Church.

In 1991 Governor Ann Richards appointed Smith to the Court of Appeals at Austin to fill Justice Bob Gammage's unexpired term as associate justice when he won election to the Supreme Court of Texas.

Justice Smith has two sons, Shannon Lyle Smith and Gregory Brixey Smith. She was formerly married to Lawrence Shannon Smith and J. Chrys Dougherty III.

photo by John Jefferson

Mack Kidd

Travis County

1991-

Mack Kidd

Mack Kidd was born in Enid, Oklahoma, January 19, 1941, to Kenneth Lee and Mary Jean Bradburn Kidd. His brother, Robert Craig Kidd, is an attorney in Houston.

Kidd moved to Houston at a young age and was graduated from Bellaire High School in 1958. He earned his bachelor of business administration from The University of Texas in 1962 and was graduated from The University of Texas School of Law in 1964. He was a member of Phi Delta Phi legal fraternity, a member of the 1963 State Bar of Texas Moot Court Championship team, and twice qualified for the National Moot Court finals.

Kidd practiced law in Austin for twenty-six years, beginning his career with the law firm of Cofer, Cofer and Hearne. Later he joined the firm of Garey, Colbert and Kidd. In 1969 he went into practice by himself and later founded a firm with current Supreme Court Justice Lloyd Doggett. The firm later became Kidd, Whitehurst, Harkness and Watson. Kidd was elected in 1991 to the Court of Appeals at Austin to fill Justice Jimmy Carroll's unexpired term as associate justice when he became chief justice.

Justice Kidd has served on the Board of Governors of the Association of Trial Lawyers of America and in 1984-85 he was president of the Texas Trial Lawyers Association. He currently serves on the national board of the American Board of Trial Advocates and the Supreme Court of Texas Task Force on Judicial Ethics.

A frequent lecturer for the State Bar of Texas and at Texas law schools, Justice Kidd has also contributed numerous seminar articles and is a regular participant in the continuing legal education program of the state bar.

He is a former president of the Association for Retarded Citizens-Austin and a former board member of the Association for Retarded Citizens-Texas. He also has served as a member of the Commissioner's Advisory Committee for the Texas Department of Mental Health and Mental Retardation.

Justice Kidd is married to Charlotte Farhar of Okeene, Oklahoma. They have three children, Kevin Kidd, Russell Roby, and Amy Roby Biggers.

MEMORIES

The preceding essays only sketch the lives of the justices on the Court of Appeals at Austin. None of them is a complete portrait. They lack the depth, breadth, judgment, and color that only a biography can supply, but as I talked to relatives of the justices and read many old newspaper accounts, I was able to gather anecdotes about some of the justices. The anecdotes give a closer look at who they were and provide a glimpse into the times in which they lived. Here are a few of the memories that remain in the hearts and minds of others.

JUSTICE WILLIAM MERCER KEY

Dr. Samuel Key, Jr., remembers his grandfather as a very kind and deliberate man, whose only weakness was an inordinate fondness for watermelon. By a remarkable coincidence, Justice Key and his family are shown in a photograph in the Austin-Travis County Collection at the Austin History Center—and they are eating watermelon with their neighbors, the Whitis family.

In a tribute to the Court of Civil Appeals in 1961, James H. Hart recalled the following story about Justice Key, who was as fond of practical jokes as he was of watermelon:

> Judge Key was especially fond of Robert H. Connerly, for many years the popular and efficient clerk of this court. Nothing pleased Judge Key more than to pull some practical joke on his friend Bob Connerly. Together with a few friends and Albert Phillips, famous camp cook, mimic, and splendid gentleman, they made numerous fishing camps on the Llano. Bob was not only a champion fisherman, but one of the State's best rifle shots. I have seen him kill quail on the wing with a .22 rifle. On one of their fishing trips to the Llano, while Bob was up the

river from camp casting for bass, Judge Key had a camp helper kill a squirrel and climb high in a nearby tree and fasten the dead squirrel firmly in a very lifelike position so that only a small part of the squirrel could be seen from the ground. When Bob returned to camp with a string of bass, Judge Key stated to Albert, in Bob's hearing, that he was getting a little tired of fish and felt like he would enjoy a good squirrel stew. Albert stated that he would be glad to fix a stew if someone would kill a squirrel, and added that he had seen a squirrel just a short time previously in a nearby tree. Bob, always wanting to please and to shoot, immediately got his .22 and he and the camp helper began looking for a squirrel. The helper soon discovered a squirrel almost entirely hidden on a high limb. In whispered tones, to prevent alarming the squirrel, it was pointed out to Bob. Bob took quick aim and fired. The squirrel did not drop. In fact, it did not move. Bob was obviously surprised. He fired a second and more deliberate shot. No results. In a subdued tone, carefully made loud enough to carry to Bob's keen ears, Judge Key remarked that obviously they had been misinformed about Bob's marksmanship, and that Albert need not yet begin the squirrel stew. Bob was so intent on bringing the meat into camp and vindicating his marksmanship that he did not catch on until he finally saw one of his many shots knock a bunch of hair from the squirrel, which still did not otherwise move. Bob's disgust was Judge Key's delight.

But on the same trip Bob got even or almost so. Judge Key's fishing equipment included a minnow trap. Minnows could enter it, but could not escape from it. With a bunch of minnows in the trap, Judge Key anchored it for the night in the river near camp. After supper it was noticed that there was lightning up the river. Judge Key, fearing that there might be a rise in the river during the night that would carry away his minnow trap, made his way to the river, picked up the trap, and slowly plodded up the river bank and carefully deposited the trap near the camp fire. In putting it down, he discovered that it was full of angry water moccasins that had invaded it for the minnows and had been unable to find an exit. In relating the incident, Bob stated that Judge Key's celerity in departing from his minnow trap would have caused envy in the fastest sprinter.

JUSTICE SAM STREETMAN

Clinton Morse of Andrews & Kurth, in his history of the law firm, wrote this about Sam Streetman as a practicing lawyer: "Many are the stories of his tactics and achievements in the courts, one of which deals with his efforts to prove an instrument a forgery through cross examination of the principal witness for the other side. After a lengthy and seemingly fruitless cross examination, and faced with apparent defeat, he abruptly asked 'Who paid you to forge this instrument?' and the witness obliged with the name."

JUSTICE JAMES HERBERT RICE

Three of Judge Rice's children, Mary Carter Rice, Elizabeth Rice Finks and Emily Rice Finch, recall that their father was at one of his cotton farms, just a few miles from Marlin, Texas, when the news came that Governor Thomas Campbell had appointed him to the court. A young man rode out to his farm in a horse and buggy to relay the news to the new appointee.

When Justice Rice accepted the appointment, he went to Austin ahead of his family and lived in the capitol during his first year on the court. He had a bedroom and bath next to his office on the second or third floor of the building.

At the end of the school year, the family followed Justice Rice to Austin so that his six remaining children could get a college education; two of his children were already in The

University of Texas. All eight children attended The University of Texas, and seven were graduated. Two sons became lawyers, and a daughter, Mary Carter Rice, became a librarian after attending Columbia University in New York and was head of the Austin Public Library for over twenty years.

In those days most of the social life in Austin centered around the governor's mansion. The governor held an open house every month, and Mrs. Rice, as wife of a justice of the Court of Civil Appeals, was expected always to be on hand as a member of the receiving line on those occasions.

Mrs. Rice, who reared eight children, was known as a hostess who was always able to set a few extra places at the table for company. In her day there were no supermarkets; instead, the grocer came to the house, took orders, and brought the purchases to the house. One vegetable supplier chalked up the family account each day on the telephone post at the end of the lawn.

During the summer in Austin a band ordinarily gave a night concert each week in Wooldridge Park. The children came too, and slid down the green sloping lawns on box tops. No one minded their shrieks and yells because the band played sufficiently loud to drown out the noise.

For many summers after the Rices moved to Austin, the Rice family would return to Marlin after the court term expired. The family would travel by train from Austin to Marlin, changing trains at Milano Junction in Milam County. Marlin was a thriving town, a spa well known for its mineral water. The water tasted "awful" in the opinion of the Rice daughters, but many others attributed great curative powers to the water when followed by a sauna.

JUSTICE CHARLES H. JENKINS

Justice Jenkins served on the board of the Brownwood School District for twenty-six years and was long remembered for his service to education in Brown County. His experience, as recounted in *Texas and Texans,* is perhaps typical of the period and provides an interesting glimpse into early school financing.

> When he first served on the board, there was a small frame building of two rooms where all the educational facilities of that community were centered. Jenkins and several of his loyal associates realized and took the lead in the matter of securing proper school buildings, not only to accommodate the immediate population but to provide and look ahead for the future. Under his leadership the board went ahead and erected a stone school house, known in that city as the "Coggin School." The finances of the city did not justify the expenditure of sufficient funds to erect such a building, and the members of the board gave their own individual notes aggregating about six thousand dollars to provide for the erection and finishing of the school. It was the second school building and the first modern building of its kind in Brownwood. The board at the same time also increased and remodeled the original school, known as the Central school, by the construction of an addition which converted the house into one of five rooms instead of two. The board went still further, secured a large plot of ground, and erected a modern high school building at a cost of sixteen thousand dollars. The city appropriated for this purpose six thousand dollars, while again the individual members of the board gave their notes to secure the balance, ten thousand dollars. These notes were subsequently paid off from year to year as the board was able to save from the school funds. Then in a few years the Central school had been outgrown, and the board determined to replace the old structure with a new at a cost of twenty thousand dollars. The city allowed the board ten thousand dollars, and once more the former process of financing was resorted to, and the board members made themselves

individually responsible for the balance of ten thousand dollars, an indebtedness which was finally cleared off in the same manner as had been done in the former case.

JUSTICE JAMES WOOTEN MCCLENDON

Justice McClendon's maternal grandfather was Dr. Absolom Christoper Columbus Thompson, a Georgia physician who spoke seven languages and was a surgeon with the Third Georgia Regiment throughout the Civil War.

As a young man, Dr. Thompson spent three years on a whaling vessel and wrote an account of his cruise and subsequent shipwreck off the coast of South America. His account was published in 1858 in the *Central Georgian* newspaper, and Justice McClendon republished the article in booklet form. It is interesting reading and a copy is included in the Austin-Travis County Collection at the Austin History Center.

When Justice McClendon was at The University of Texas, Congress Avenue was unpaved, the street railway system was quite new, there were approximately four hundred students enrolled at the university (153 in the law department), and Austin was a city of 17,000 residents. The license fee for an attorney was ten dollars a year, five dollars in state tax and two dollars and fifty cents in county and city tax. A dam across the Colorado River was newly completed in 1893 and it was a local source of humor that the people of Austin had practically gone "dam crazy."

While a law student, McClendon was part of a student "uprising" that established March 2d, Texas Independence Day, as a school holiday. Today March 2d is not an official school holiday, but it is still celebrated by students and faculty on campus with a gathering on the mall—complete with cake, Texas flag, a speech from the university president, and the traditional cannon.

In 1897 members of the senior law class asked President George T. Winston for a school holiday on March 2d to celebrate Texas Independence Day, but President Winston, having arrived recently from North Carolina, did not like the idea. Led by J.W. McClendon and others, the seniors revolted, seized a cannon at the capitol, and dragged it back to the campus. Patriotic speeches were made and the cannon fired several times. Judge J.C. Townes and Judge R.L. Batts of the law faculty accepted invitations to make speeches and with some difficulty the students persuaded President Winston to appear at the celebration, at which he made the following remarks: "I was born in the land of liberty, nursed on the bottle of liberty, rocked in the cradle of liberty, and grew up a son of liberty, but the students at The University of Texas take more liberties than any group I have ever seen." But he gave them their holiday.

Justice McClendon loved to tell the story about how his mother was accepted for missionary work. After the death of his father, his mother—always interested in mission work—decided to become a missionary. When the Woman's Board of Missions of the Methodist Episcopal Church, South met in 1889 in Little Rock, Arkansas, his mother and a friend traveled to Little Rock to offer themselves as missionaries. She was told: "Mrs. McClendon, you must think we are crazy if you think we would send a widow with five children away to some mission." She replied, "May I have the floor for ten minutes?" and at the end of her speech the Board promptly voted unanimously to sponsor her as a missionary.

At the time of his death, Justice McLendon was already planning his 100th birthday party at Westwood County Club (which incorporates a part of McClendon's former home), intending to invite "anyone who thinks he's a friend of mine."

JUSTICE MALLORY BENTON BLAIR

Like Justice Key, Blair was an avid fisherman. When asked to go fishing, the Justice liked to reply, "Well, I doubt if I can go before about twenty minutes from now."

His daughter, Sarah Margaret Doughtery, remembers a time when her father went through a very emotional time when he was district judge. He had sentenced a man to death in a murder trial and it caused him to have sunken eyes with dark circles around them. It worried him a great deal, and Sarah remembers that a gallows was erected in the middle of town, which only served to remind him of the consequences of his sentence. The trial worried the community, too, because there was a faction that thought the verdict was justified and a faction that thought otherwise.

JUSTICE ROY COLMAN ARCHER

Judge Archer came from a remarkably prolific family. He and his twenty brothers and sisters reared a total of one hundred and fifty-eight children. Nine of his brothers and sisters had ten or more children.

Justice Archer loved to tell stories. A family history, *The Legacy of John McQuatty Archer,* contains the following, related by Justice Archer:

> In the winter of 1899, when I was nine years of age, my father moved the whole family to the Panhandle. We moved with seven wagons of family goods including the farming equipment and three-hundred head of horses that my father had traded land for. We had a tent and carried an iron stove (just four walls and a top to it) for heating and cooking.
>
> There was very little to do in the Panhandle to make a living and everybody there was in about the same shape. In the winter of 1903 there fell a big snow and in fact in years to come it was called the winter of the big snow. I recall it being about five foot deep on the level. Thousands of cattle died. Some of the Archer boys got a job skinning the frozen cattle and received half of the hides they took. We sold the hides in Canadian (Texas) and made enough for my father, John M., to pay off some of his debts.
>
> The county was organized by my father and some

others. Billy Dixon, the famous Indian fighter who later won the Congressional Medal of Honor, was elected sheriff. For some reason he was found not eligible to serve and he moved away, down on the Canadian River.

One time my brother Bob and I got a job keeping stragglers up when the Turkey Track Ranch moved its herds to New Mexico. The stragglers were cattle that had gotten lost from the herd or were sickly, or had given birth to new calves. There were three herds of about 1500 head each. We were paid $30 a month and our food—just like the men on the drive were paid. We drove the herd to a ranch the other side of Albuquerque and were paid off in gold. On our way back home we stopped in Tularosa, and bought a little canned stuff and showed the store keeper our gold—being very proud of it. We went on eight or ten miles to a water hole to spend the night. Just about dark up rode the man from Tularosa with another man who claimed he was the Post Master and that they were both federal officers. The two men arrested Bob and me for robbing the post office and taking the gold.

The two men took us to a ranch house not too far away to spend the night. The ranch was owned by an Anglo woman and her Mexican husband whose name was DeAlavara. Later that night another man came in. The place seemed to be a central gathering place. The next morning we were still pretty scared and were ready to compromise and give the two men the gold and for them to let us go. The other man who had come to the ranch the night before said to one of the men who had arrested us, "Let me see your appointment as Post Master." The other man, who was with the one claiming to be the Post Master said, "Listen, I'm getting out of this damned thing. I didn't have anything to do with it." The man who had come in late said, "Well, I'm the post office examiner and I am on the way to examine your post office right now and I can tell from the sale of stamps and reports how much money you had." The man admitted that he didn't have any money and we didn't steal any money.

Bob and I were subpoenaed a few weeks later to go to Santa Fe as witnesses. Since we were minors we were allowed to have some caretakers along, so we and three of our brothers set out for Santa Fe. Bob and I were paid two dollars a day each as witness fees and each of us (all five) was paid two dollars a day for expenses. It took three weeks to go by wagon from Hutchinson County to Santa Fe, New Mexico. About three days after we got there the two men pleaded guilty so we didn't have to testify. We went back home. The gold and unused expense money was used to pay the state some funds to keep our land.

Although land was very cheap in the Panhandle —fifty cents an acre for grass land and a dollar an acre for farming land—the terms were good, two cents an acre down and four years to pay—it was still hard to come up with the cash to make the payments. In addition to skinning carcasses, helping in cattle drives and the like, another way was trading. John M. loved to trade - he was good at it and would give two or three of his boys some horses and tell them to go trade. He would say, "I don't care what you trade for, just don't bring these same horses back."

One of the favorite trading places was with the Indians in the "Oklahoma Strip." These Indians had been given some very good horses by the government. The only thing was, the horses had been branded "US" and it was against the law to buy or sell them. The Indians, no dummies, would hide out the best colts and not let them be branded so they could sell or trade them as they pleased. The Archer

> boys often would come to trade.
>
> The Indian horses were faster than those owned by the Archers. They would all get into a bragging contest about whose was the fastest and a horse race with side bets would be arranged. The race would be a quarter to a half mile long or maybe further. The rules were that the two riders would come to the start line at full gallop. There were two "seconds" at the start line—one an Indian and the other an Archer (usually me). The purpose of the "seconds" was to see that the horses were about even at the start. Ben weighed the least and he was usually the rider. He was instructed by his brothers to pull up his horse just before he got to the starting line so that the Indian pony crossed the line several yards ahead. I would call out "foul" and they would have to restart. The Indian pony would be on the dead run and would go quite a little ways before he could be stopped and turned around. After a couple of false starts, the Indian pony would be pretty well pooped and Ben would make a proper start and win. After the race the Archer boys would collect their winnings and leave as quickly as they could before the Indians caught on to what they had done.

JUSTICE C. K. RICHARDS

In a memorial tribute to Justice Richards on February 25, 1966, James R. Norvell, Association Justice of the Supreme Court of Texas, had this to say about Richards and practicing law in the Rio Grande Valley in the 1920s and 30s.

> It has been almost forty years now since I became acquainted with Judge C.K. Richards. He came to the Rio Grande Valley of Texas about a year before I did. Both of us were then young men. At that time Judge Richards was practicing law in Brownsville in

association with Joseph K. Wells, a son of James B. Wells, one of the prominent political figures of South Texas, and long-time attorney for the King Ranch interests.

The Rio Grande Valley in the twenties and early thirties was highly attractive to a young lawyer who was interested in the trial practice. The counties of Hidalgo and Cameron were undergoing a period of ferment. People from practically all the States in the Union had come to the section as a result of the activities of various land selling companies who ran excursions into the Valley and sold thousands of acres of land to non-residents of Texas. These land purchasers proved to be a highly litigious group. Regardless of whatever recourse they may have had in their home communities upon feeling aggrieved, when they found themselves in a new and unfamiliar country with a nation-wide economic depression facing them, they looked upon the courthouse as a shadow of a rock in a weary land, so to speak. They were ready to sue. This situation made good business for lawyers although an extensive trial practice in those times did not necessarily mean that the lawyer's financial returns would be correspondingly renumerative. It was in this background and under these circumstances that I like best to remember Judge Richards. I do not recall that we ever sat on the same side of the table in any lawsuit. I represented a number of insolvent municipalities at the time. I recall that we put one school district through municipal bankruptcy under an Act of Congress adopted to meet the grave emergencies of the depression. In this species of litigation, I met Judge Richards as an opposing advocate, and so it came about that it was as a persistent antagonist in the courtroom that I learned to respect him and to love him. It was not through his gentleness in dealing

> with me as a somewhat younger lawyer that I learned to admire him. While he was always fair to his opponents and would treat them with respect and decency as long as they would permit it, I would not say he overwhelmed one with compassion and graciousness in the adversary proceeding that we know as a lawsuit. I do not recall that any judge experienced any difficulty in ascertaining which side of the case he represented. To C.K. Richards, the trial of a cause was a joyous call to battle.

JUSTICE TRUEMAN EDGAR O'QUINN

Bill Fowler, a former law clerk, greatly admired Judge O'Quinn and described him as a true Southern gentleman. The two qualities Fowler admired most were Justice O'Quinn's courage— he was never afraid to sign his name to an opinion he knew might not be popular with the bar or the public—and his love and use of the English language. In "The Judge's Collection," Dr. Jenny Lind Porter writes,

> His war on bad grammar and mangled Latin became so well known around the court that some lawyers would call the Clerk of the Court, Mrs. Margie Love, before a session and ask how to pronounce a Latin word or phrase so that Justice O'Quinn wouldn't correct them.
>
> The Judge had over the years become so identified with O. Henry in the minds of the public that once, after hearing O'Quinn talk about O. Henry, the *American Statesman* Editor Charles E. Green wrote in his column, "O. Henry said O'Quinn spent three years in prison for embezzlement." By the time the Bulldog Edition of the paper hit the streets, Charlie Green was on the telephone, apologizing. A correction would appear in the afternoon edition. The newspaper's attorneys

would be in touch with Trueman.

"Quit worrying," laughed the judge. "Everybody knows I was never in the penitentiary. I've been in Austin since 1922!"

Howard Sartin—whose father, Guy, married O. Henry's daughter Margaret, says that "If you don't know Judge O'Quinn, you must meet him. He looks like John Huston, the motion picture director, and talks the way all little boys dream that tall Texans should talk. Trueman can spin tales tall or short, with the best there ever was. If he's *agin* something, he takes a second look. But if he's *fer* it, the devil better move over,'cause nothing will deter him. O'Quinn is *fer* O. Henry."

JUSTICE ROBERT O. "BOB" SMITH

To demonstrate Justice Smith's dry wit, John Allen, Smith's former law partner, told this story in a 1961 newspaper article:

> When Bob was in the district attorney's office, he was prosecuting a habitual criminal.Now the only sentence for someone tried and convicted as an habitual criminal is life imprisonment. The boy had been in the pen twice in Texas and twice in California. He sat reading the Bible all through the trial.
>
> The jury came back with a life sentence. The boy turned to Bob and said "Mr. Smith, you're a mean man but I've been praying for you."
>
> Bob said, "Joe, from the kind of help you've been getting from your prayers, I'd count it a favor if you wouldn't even mention my name."